Bible Prayers
for Bedtime

Jane Landreth

Illustrated by Richard Hoit

© 2008 by Barbour Publishing, Inc.

Manuscript written and prepared in association with Snapdragon Group℠ Tulsa, Oklahoma, USA.

All rights reserved. No part of this publication may be reproduced or transmitted for commercial purposes, except for brief quotations in printed reviews, without written permission of the publisher.

Churches and other noncommercial interests may reproduce portions of this book without the express written permission of Barbour Publishing, provided that the text does not exceed 500 words or 5 percent of the entire book, whichever is less and that the text is not material quoted from another publisher. When reproducing text from this book, include the following credit line: "From *Bible Prayers for Bedtime*, published by Barbour Publishing, Inc. Used by permission."

All scripture quotations, unless otherwise noted, are taken from the Holy Bible: New International Version®. niv®. Copyright 1973, 1978, 1984 by International Bible Society. Used by permission of Zondervan. All rights reserved.

Scripture quotations marked ncv are taken from the New Century Version®. Copyright © 2005 by Thomas Nelson, Inc. Used by permission. All rights reserved.

Cover and interior illustrations by Richard Hoit

Published by Barbour Publishing, Inc., P. O. Box 719, Uhrichsville, Ohio 44683, www.barbourbooks.com

Our mission is to publish and distribute inspirational products offering exceptional value and biblical encouragement to the masses.

Printed in China.

When a believing
person prays,
great things happen.

JAMES 5:16 NCV

"Speak to Me, Lord"

"Samuel! Samuel!"

Samuel said, "Speak, for your servant is listening."
1 Samuel 3:10

Praying isn't always talking to God. Sometimes we need to be quiet and listen. Young Samuel learned to listen to God.

Samuel yawned and stretched his arms. He was sleepy, so he lay down and closed his eyes. Then Samuel heard someone call.

"Samuel! Samuel!"

He jumped out of bed and ran to where Eli, the priest, slept. "You called me, and here I am," Samuel said.

Eli looked surprised. "I did not call you," he said. "Go back to bed."

Samuel went back to bed. Then he

heard the voice again.

"Samuel! Samuel!"

Samuel hurried to Eli. "Did you call me?" he asked.

"No," said Eli. "I did not call you. Go back to bed."

Samuel was just closing his eyes when he heard the voice again.

"Samuel! Samuel!"

He ran to Eli for the third time. "Did you call me?"

Then Eli knew God was calling Samuel. "When you hear the voice again," Eli told

Samuel, "say, 'Speak to me, God. I am listening.'"

Soon Samuel heard the voice again.

"Samuel! Samuel!"

Samuel said, "Speak to me, God. I am listening."

Then something wonderful happened. God spoke to Samuel. And Samuel listened carefully to all God told him.

God, thank You for listening to the things I want to tell You. Help me to be quiet and listen to the things You want to tell me. Amen.

One, Two, Three Times

Three times each day Daniel would kneel down to pray
and thank God, just as he always had done.
DANIEL 6:10 NCV

God hears us every time we pray. Daniel prayed—one, two, three times—every day, and God heard his prayer each time.

The king gave Daniel an important job. But some men did not like Daniel. They were jealous. They thought of a plan to get Daniel in trouble.

The men told the king, "Let's make a new rule. Everyone must pray to you." The king thought this rule was a good idea. He told the people they must pray only to him.

The next day, Daniel prayed to God—one,

two, three times—just as he always did. The men, who were watching Daniel, ran to tell the king what they had seen.

The king was sad he had made the new rule. The men had tricked him. Now he had to throw Daniel into the lions' cage for disobeying the new rule.

The lions went *r-r-roar!* They were very hungry. *R-r-roar!*

But Daniel was not afraid. He knew God would take care of him.

The next morning the king came to the lions' cage. Daniel called out, "King,

I am safe. God took care of me! He sent an angel to shut the lions' mouths."

The king made a new rule. Everyone should pray only to God.

> Dear God, help me to remember to pray when I'm afraid. Keep me safe when I'm in trouble. Thank You for hearing my prayer every time I pray. Amen.

Praying Anywhere

From inside the fish
Jonah prayed to the Lord his God.
Jonah 2:1

We can pray anywhere. Jonah prayed to God in many places—even from the inside of a fish!

One day God told Jonah, "Go to the town of Nineveh. Tell the people they have disobeyed Me."

Jonah had always obeyed God. But this time he disobeyed. Instead of going to Nineveh, he decided to get on a boat and go far away in the other direction.

Suddenly the sky turned black and strong winds blew. The waves crashed. The men on the boat were afraid. But

Jonah knew God had sent the storm because he had disobeyed.

Jonah told the men, "Throw me into the sea and the storm will stop."

One, two, three! The men threw Jonah into the water. Sure enough, the waves stopped crashing. The boat was safe.

Then God sent a huge fish. The fish opened its mouth wide and *WHOOSH!* Jonah was in the belly of the big fish!

Jonah began to pray. "God, forgive me for disobeying."

When God brought the big fish close

to land, it began to cough. *AACK!*—it coughed Jonah right onto the beach.

Then God talked to Jonah. "Now it's time to take my message to Nineveh!" And this time, Jonah obeyed!

Dear God, thank You for hearing me when I pray at home, at school, or at church. I can pray anywhere, and You will hear me. Amen.

Loaves and Fish

(Jesus) took the five loaves and the two fish and, looking to heaven, he thanked God for the food.
Matthew 14:19 NCV

God wants us to thank Him for the food we eat—just like Jesus did.

Jesus and His disciples sat down to rest on a hillside one day. Before they knew it, a lot of people had gathered around. They wanted Jesus to tell them about God.

Jesus started to teach them. Soon, many people were sitting on the grassy hill, listening to Him. They listened until suppertime. They didn't even notice they were hungry until Jesus stopped talking.

"We should send these people home so they can eat supper," Jesus' disciples said to Him.

But Jesus said to His disciples, "They are too far from home. We must give them something to eat."

"What?" the disciples said. "We don't have any food!"

Just then Andrew said, "This little boy says he wants to share his supper. But it is only five little loaves of bread and two fish. It is enough to feed only a few."

Jesus took the little boy's supper and

thanked God for the food. Then He began to break the bread and fish into pieces. Soon there were hundreds and hundreds of pieces of bread and fish—enough to feed all the hungry people.

God, thank You for giving me food to eat. Help me to share my food with those who are hungry. Amen.

Praying is talking to God, just like you would talk to anyone else. God wants to know the things you need. But He also wants to know the fun things you do. Jesus' disciples wanted to know how to pray, and Jesus taught them.

Jesus spent much time praying to God. Sometimes He would stay awake all night to pray. Sometimes Jesus would find a quiet spot where He could talk to God.

Jesus' special helpers, the disciples, saw Jesus pray many times. One day when Jesus had finished praying, one of the disciples came to Him. The disciple said, "Jesus, teach *us* how to pray."

Jesus told His helpers that they could talk to God the same way they talked to their fathers here on earth.

Jesus said, "When you pray, call God, 'Father.' Tell Him you love Him. Ask Him for the food you need each day. Ask Him to forgive the wrong things you do. Tell Him that you will forgive people who have done bad things to you. Ask Him to help you do what is right."

Jesus was happy because His disciples

wanted to know how to talk to God. He is happy when you talk to God, too!

Father, thank You for listening to me when I pray. I'm glad I can tell You what I need, but I'm also happy I can tell You about the fun things, too. Amen.

Do you remember to thank God for making you well after you have been sick? A sick man, who was made well, almost forgot to thank Jesus.

There was a man who had sores all over his body. He was sad because he had to leave his family and go to a place where nine other sick men lived.

One day, Jesus came down the road. "Please make us well!" the sick men called out to Jesus.

Jesus saw the sores on the men's hands and feet. "Go and show yourselves to the helpers at the temple," He said.

The ten men were happy! They ran down the road toward town. Suddenly, they looked at their hands and feet. The sores were gone! Jesus had made them well.

The men ran faster toward the temple—all but one man. He stopped and ran back to Jesus. The man got down on his knees in front of Jesus. He said, "Thank You for making me well!"

Jesus looked at the man and said, "I'm glad you came back to thank Me. Go home to your family. You knew I could make you well and I did."

Dear heavenly Father, whenever I am sick, help me to remember to thank You for making me well again. Amen.

Praying and Singing

About midnight Paul and Silas were praying
and singing hymns to God.
Acts 16:25

God hears our prayers, no matter where we are or what time it is. Paul and Silas knew God heard their prayers—even in jail in the middle of the night.

One day, Paul and Silas were telling people about Jesus. Some people were glad to hear about Jesus, but others became angry. They shouted, "Put Paul and Silas in jail! Do not let them out!"

The jailer put Paul and Silas in the back of the jail. He put chains around their hands and feet. They could hardly move. It was very dark and quiet.

In the middle of the night, Paul and Silas prayed. They began to sing praises to God. The prayers made Paul and Silas happy. The songs made them happy, too.

Suddenly, there were loud noises! *Bang! Crash!* Everything began to shake. It was an earthquake! The earthquake popped open the jail doors. It shook loose the chains around Paul and Silas.

The jailer was afraid. "Paul and Silas have escaped!" he yelled.

But Paul said, "We're still here." Then Paul and Silas told the jailer about Jesus.

Paul and Silas were happy because God had heard their prayers and their singing—even in jail in the middle of the night!

Dear Jesus, thank You for being near me at all times. Help me remember to pray and sing praises to You wherever I am and at anytime— day or night. Amen.

Dear God, I'm so glad that I can talk to You. Thank You for listening to my prayers! Amen.